# GREAT MINDS
## of Ancient Science and Math

# THE FATHER OF THE ATOM

## DEMOCRITUS AND THE NATURE OF MATTER

Katherine Macfarlane

**Enslow Publishers, Inc.**
40 Industrial Road
Box 398
Berkeley Heights, NJ 07922
USA

http://www.enslow.com

*To my father*
*L. Wayland Macfarlane*

**Library of Congress Cataloging-in-Publication Data**

Macfarlane, Katherine.
   The father of the atom : Democritus and the nature of matter / Katherine Macfarlane.
      p. cm. — (Great minds of ancient science and math)
   Summary: "A biography of ancient Greek philosopher Democritus, who believed that all matter was made up of indivisible and indestructible particles called atoms moving around in a void"—Provided by publisher.
   Includes bibliographical references and index.
   ISBN-13: 978-0-7660-3410-5
   ISBN-10: 0-7660-3410-0
   1. Atoms—Juvenile literature. 2. Matter—Constitution—Junvenile literature. 3. Democritus, ca. 460–ca. 370 B.C.—Juvenile literature. 4. Mathematics, Ancient—Greece—Juvenile literature. I. Title.
QC173.16.M33 2010
539.7—dc22

                        2008046265

Printed in the United States of America

10 9 8 7 6 5 4 3 2 1

**To Our Readers:** We have done our best to make sure all Internet addresses in this book were active and appropriate when we went to press. However, the author and the publisher have no control over and assume no liability for the material available on those Internet sites or on other Web sites they may link to. Any comments or suggestions can be sent by e-mail to comments@enslow.com or to the address on the back cover.

♻ Enslow Publishers, Inc., is committed to printing our books on recycled paper. The paper in every book contains 10% to 30% post-consumer waste (PCW). The cover board on the outside of each book contains 100% PCW. Our goal is to do our part to help young people and the environment too!

**Illustration Credits:** Cordelia Molloy/Photo Researchers, Inc., p. 41; David Nicholls/Photo Researchers, Inc., p. 86; Enslow Publishers, Inc., p. 10; Everrett Collection, Inc., pp. 6, 20, 30; Filip Miletic/Shutterstock Images LLC, p. 85; Jupiterimages Corporation, pp. 75, 80, 81, 82, 84; Laguna Design/Photo Researchers, Inc., p. 87; Mary Evans Picture Library/Everett Collection, p. 64; Michel Grenet/Photo Researchers, Inc., p. 67; Scala/Art Resource, NY, p. 26; Science Source/Photo Researchers, Inc., p. 14; The Granger Collection, New York, p. 31; The Image Works, p. 12; Wikipedia, p. 61.

**Cover Illustration:** An imagined likeness of Democritus by seventeenth-century painter Jusepe de Ribera, © Collection of the Earl of Pembroke, Wilton House, Wilts./The Bridgeman Art Library.

# CONTENTS

# 1

# THE LIFE AND TIMES OF DEMOCRITUS

THE YOUNG MAN STALKING ALONG THE waterfront of the Piraeus, the seaport of Athens, was clearly in a rage. His beard curled tightly and aggressively, and the face visible above the beard was fixed in a scowl. His thick eyebrows drew down over his eyes, which were dark and peering. Even his tightly curled hair had an aggressive look to it. Behind him a slave struggled along with his baggage.

The young man came to a stop, turned, and barked. The slave dropped the baggage at his master's feet and hurried away along the waterfront. The young man sat down on his bundles (the better to keep thieving Athenian hands out of them, he muttered to himself), folded his arms, and glared about him.

A portrait of Democritus (c. 460–370 B.C.), the Greek philosopher who would pioneer atomic theory.

He had not enjoyed his stay in Athens.[1] For one thing, he was amazed that no one in this city had ever heard of him, *Democritus*! Worse yet, no one had ever heard of his teacher Leucippus. Did they think the only philosophers worth studying were in Athens? Like that infernal pest Socrates? Clearly these Athenians had a very good opinion of themselves. If he heard once more that Athens was the jewel of Greece and the queen of philosophical learning, he was going to take his fists to the man who said it.

As for how Athens was the savior of Greece twice over from the Persian barbarians, well, in Democritus's opinion, these people just did not know how to get along with Persians. Had not his own father Hegesistratus entertained the Persian King Xerxes in his own home, like a good Abderite citizen, and found him a pleasant and generous guest? Had Xerxes not left Hegesistratus some of his own Persian and Babylonian wise men to educate Democritus and his brothers?

Then there was Anaxagoras. Democritus had made this trip to Athens on purpose to speak with Anaxagoras. He wanted to discuss with the

7

old philosopher some questions Leucippus had about Anaxagoras's theory of seeds, and how there could be seeds of everything in everything. But Anaxagoras had refused to see him! He had turned him away from his door with some trumped-up excuse about being too old to receive guests. He had claimed his joints ached too much, that he had no desire but to sit by a warm brazier and finish his writing before the Merciful One carried him off. To make matters worse, Anaxagoras's doorkeeper had made fun of Democritus's clothes, especially the way he bundled his mantle about himself like a blanket, instead of draping it so that one end trailed elegantly in the Athenian manner. He had told him he looked liked an Abderite. Democritus was, in fact, from Abdera, and he found the fellow's remarks infuriating. What did the oaf *expect* him to look like? (Among the Greeks, and even among the Romans, Abdera was regarded as a backwater, and Abderites had a reputation for being provincial and stupid. To call someone an Abderite, whether or not they were from

Abdera, was an insult. But Democritus, being from Abdera, did not know that.)

At that moment the slave came panting up and told Democritus that he had found a ship bound for Abdera, and it would be leaving at the fifth hour. Democritus left him to deal with the baggage and transferred his glare to an Athenian householder with a market basket over his arm, bargaining with a fisherman for his catch of octopus. The thought of seafood made Democritus's stomach rumble. He could smell the odor of fresh bread wafting from a waterfront tavern, and thought longingly of olives and hard-boiled eggs and warm bread dipped in olive oil and salt. He wondered if he could squeeze in breakfast before catching his ship home to Abdera.

Democritus, the young man who left Athens in such an outraged frame of mind, was one of the latest of many inquiring Greek minds that are known today as the pre-Socratic philosophers. They are called this because most of them lived before Socrates, the most famous of the Greek philosophers. The pre-Socratics were the

first to raise questions about how the universe came to be and what matter is made of.

In the 400s B.C., Greece was a hotbed of philosophy—literally, "love of wisdom." For the first time thinking people broke free of unquestioning belief in myths about the gods, and sought answers to universal questions on their own. Many different schools of philosophy arose, not only on mainland Greece, but also on the coast of Asia Minor (now Turkey), the Greek islands, and even as far away as the Greek colonies in southern Italy and Sicily. One of these schools, the atomists, arose in Abdera, a

Greek colony in a region north of Greece called Thrace. The atomists taught that everything is made of atoms, minute particles of matter, in various combinations.

Democritus was not the first of the atomist philosophers, but he was the most influential. He was born in Abdera around 460 B.C., and died there around 370 B.C.[2] The ninety years he lived spanned the Golden Age of Greece, between the end of the wars with Persia around 465 B.C. and the rise of the Macedonian Empire under Philip II of Macedonia and Alexander the Great, beginning around 360 B.C. This period saw great architectural masterpieces built, such as the Parthenon in Athens and the temple of Zeus at Olympia. Sculptors like Myron, Phidias, and Praxiteles produced their greatest works in bronze and marble. The tragedies of Sophocles and Euripides were written and performed, as were the comedies of Aristophanes. The product of speculation and inquiry that we know as Greek philosophy culminated in the teachings of Socrates and Plato. It is no wonder that the atomists of Abdera were somewhat overshadowed.

This famous statuette of Socrates—a Hellenistic copy probably from a contemporary portrait or a post-mortem carving by a sculptor who knew Socrates (who was himself a sculptor)—is kept in the British Museum.

Leucippus, the first of the known atomist philosophers, settled in Abdera sometime around 450 B.C., and Democritus became his student. Although Democritus was not the first to develop the atomic theory, he expanded and systematized Leucippus's teachings. Leucippus must have filled Democritus with a deep love of learning, for he devoted the rest of his life to exploring the world and learning what he could from other philosophers.

According to Diogenes Laertius, the third-century biographer who tells us the most about Democritus's life (although today he is not considered terribly reliable), Democritus traveled to Athens as a young man, where he was very annoyed to find that no one there had ever heard of him.[3] He was especially annoyed that Anaxagoras, a famous philosopher who was living in Athens at the time, would not grant him a visit, in spite of the fact that Anaxagoras had expounded theories that may have inspired atomism. Both Democritus and his teacher Leucippus must have been highly interested in Anaxagoras's teachings.[4]

Leucippus was Democritus's teacher and the originator of atomism, the theory that everything is made up of indivisible particles called atoms. Little is known about his life, but his ideas were preserved and expanded upon by Democritus.

From Athens, Democritus returned to Abdera, and until the death of his father, pursued his studies with Leucippus. After his father's death the estate was divided equally among Democritus and his two brothers. Democritus's share came to more than a hundred talents, a considerable fortune.[5]

With his share of the estate in hand, Democritus set off to explore the world. According to Diogenes Laertius, he spent some time in Egypt, where he studied mathematics with the priests there (what he would have studied was probably geometry, which originated in Egypt). Thereafter he traveled to Persia, where he studied with the magi (Persian wise men). He was already familiar with their teachings from studying with some magi and Chaldeans (Babylonian wise men) that the Persian king Xerxes had left with Democritus's father in return for his hospitality. He probably reached Babylon, and may have gone as far as the Persian Gulf.[6]

From Persia, Democritus may even have traveled to India and studied with the gymnosophists (literally, "naked wise men").[7] They practiced asceticism (self-denial); ate little; wore only a loincloth; avoided meat, alcohol, and sexual relationships; and meditated. Gymnosophy may have been an early form of yoga.

From India, Democritus may have returned to Abdera by way of Ethiopia, where there was supposed to be another school of ascetic philosophers.[8]

Democritus arrived back in Abdera with his fortune spent, and was forced to accept the support of his brother Damasus. He devoted himself to study and to writing his teachings. He wrote many books, of which nothing has survived except fragments quoted by other authors. Democritus's books from which quotations survive are *The Great World System* (which may actually have been written by Leucippus, or by Democritus and Leucippus working together), *The Little World System,* and *On Mind.*[9]

Democritus became greatly respected in Abdera. His fellow citizens called him "Wisdom."

He lived to a great old age, some sources say one hundred nine. It is most likely, however, that he died around 370 B.C., at the age of ninety. His fellow Abderites gave him a public funeral, paid for by the state, which was a great honor.[10]

# 2

# WHAT IS MATTER MADE OF?

PEOPLE HAVE ALWAYS WONDERED HOW the world came to be. Many early people had elaborate myths about who or what made the world and everything in it. The early Greeks were no exception. The poet Hesiod, in an epic poem called *Theogony* (The Origin of the Gods), describes how the primal Chaos gave birth to the goddess Gaia (Earth), from whom sprang Ouranos (the Heavens) and everything else in the universe.[1]

However, around the middle of the 500s B.C., a school of thought grew up that rejected the ancient Greek myths about the origin of the universe and the deeds of the Olympian gods. These men tried to explore and explain how the world functions through their own observation and analysis. They have become known as the pre-Socratic philosophers, because they lived and taught before the time of Socrates, the most famous of the Greek philosophers.

Thales was the first of the pre-Socratic philosophers to question the myth of how the universe came to be. He lived in the Greek city of Miletos, on the coast of Asia Minor, and became the founder of the Milesian school of philosophy. One of the most important questions the Milesian philosophers asked was "What is matter made of?" They tried to determine whether matter had a basic material, or *archê* (ar-KAY), out of which everything else was formed. Even more important, while they might consider the archê divine, they believed that it operated according to natural laws, not the sort of whims inflicted on humans by the Olympian gods. Once people figured out how these natural laws operated, they would know what to expect from the natural world. Unfortunately, that task was not as easy as the Milesian philosophers thought. People today are

Thales founded the Milesian school of philosophy around 550 B.C. They theorized about what the physical world was made of and came up with the concept of archê, primal matter.

still coming to grips with how the natural world operates— global warming is one modern example of this.

Although most of the Milesian philosophers taught and wrote a great deal, none of their original works have survived. What we know about them comes from quotations from later philosophers. Some of these are famous, for example Aristotle, a student of Plato and an exhaustive encyclopedist. Others are preserved in quotations from still later philosophers.

If Thales wrote any books of his own, they have not survived. What we know about him comes mostly from the writings of the much later

Greek philosopher Aristotle. According to Aristotle, "Thales, the founder of this type of philosophy, says the principle [that is, the archê] is water."[2] This is not as surprising as it sounds at first. Is not water the only substance that can be a solid, a liquid, and a vapor under normal conditions? Could not it therefore be the primal substance out of which, under the right conditions, all matter is formed? Thales also noted that a moist environment is necessary for all living things to be nurtured and come into being, whether plants or animals or humans.

Thales's student Anaximander proposed an archê that was not water but a sort of primal soup he called "the Indefinite" or "the Infinite." Out of the Indefinite all forms of matter arise, and in time are dissolved back into the Indefinite.[3] This Indefinite was like no known form of matter, although it formed the basis for all of them. Aristotle describes it as "being thicker than air and fire and finer than the others," that is, water and earth,[4] or possibly a mixture of all the elements.[5]

Anaximenes, another of the Milesians and a colleague of Anaximander, rejected Anaximander's theory of the Indefinite, and taught that the archê was air. As Simplicius, a later philosopher (A.D. 500s), explains, "Anaximenes . . . says that the underlying nature is . . . not undefined as Anaximander said but definite, for he identifies it as air; and it differs in its substantial nature by rarity [thinness] and density. Being made finer it becomes fire, being made thicker it becomes wind, then cloud, then (when thickened still more) water, then earth, then stones; and the rest come into being from these."[6] Anaximenes believed that when matter became more dense it became cold, and when it became more rarified it became hot,[7] a remarkable insight for someone with no concept of atomic theory.

One of the most baffling of the pre-Socratic philosophers is Heraclitus of Ephesus. He was not one of the Milesians, although he certainly knew about them. He does not seem to have allied himself with any philosophical school, but operated along his own lines. His one book seems to have been a collection of epigrams or sayings; he is said to have written in an "oracular" style, which suggests riddles or word puzzles. The surviving fragments of his writings tend to bear this out. He is known for the statement, *panta chorei*, "all things flow," which seems to mean that he saw the universe in a constant state of change or flux, and for the observation that "You cannot step twice into the same river." By this he appears to mean that while both you and the river retain the same shape, both you and the water in the river are constantly changing.[8] The water flows and the flow changes the river bed.

One of the fragments of Heraclitus suggests that he considered the archê to be fire: "The same world of all things, neither any of the gods, nor any one of men, made. But there was, and is, and will be ever-living fire, kindled according to measure, and quenched according to measure."[9]

If this is so, then his worldview may not have been that different from that of Thales and Anaximenes. One addition that Heraclitus did make to the thought of his time was that the universe was ruled by a *logos* (literally, "word").[10]

This is not quite the same *logos* that the Gospel of John refers to in the original Greek Bible ("In the beginning was the Word . . ."), but rather a sort of natural law or schematic that governed how the universe operated. The logos was immortal and unchanging, and human beings could, if they tried hard enough, eventually understand it. This seems to be another idea that he borrowed from the Milesian philosophers.

Parmenides, founder of the Eleatic school of philosophy (about 510 B.C. to sometime after 450 B.C.), proposed a worldview that appears to be nearly the opposite of what Heraclitus taught. Whereas Heraclitus envisioned a universe constantly changing, Parmenides saw Reality, or What Is, as changeless. He expresses his philosophical theories in a poem called *On Nature,* which consists of two parts and an introduction or proem. The two parts following the proem, in which he is instructed by an unnamed goddess on the nature of reality, he calls "The Way of Truth" and "The Way of Opinion." "The Way of Truth"  has survived almost intact, perhaps because it was such a powerful influence on later philosophers, notably Plato; "The Way of Opinion" exists only in fragmentary form, but there is enough of it left that scholars can get a general idea of what Parmenides had to say on the subject.

In "The Way of Truth" Parmenides' goddess reveals that Reality, or What Is, is uncreated and deathless, since What Is cannot come into being from What Is Not, or ever change into What Is Not. It is also whole and uniform, inviolate—that is, incapable of being changed—and therefore perfect. It is still and motionless; all appearances of matter in motion are just that: appearances, and illusory. Parmenides concludes that What Is cannot be perceived by the senses, but only by reason, or logos. What is perceived by the senses is only opinion, or *doxa*; that is, all perceptions are mere appearance or illusion.[11] It is odd that having issued the admonition, "Here I end my trustworthy discourse and thought concerning truth; henceforth learn the beliefs of mortal men, listening to the deceitful ordering of my words."[12]

Parmenides (c. 510–450 B.C.) founded the Eleatic school of philosophy, which tried to explain the world using logical arguments.

Parmenides apparently did not devote the second part of his poem to an explanation of how human senses function and how it is possible for humans to perceive creation and change and destruction when no such things existed. Instead he seemingly went into an extensive description of cosmology (how the sun, moon, and stars operate, or at least seem to) and a discussion of how living things reproduce (or seem to), without any explanation of how all this appears to take place when in fact nothing of the sort is actually happening. Perhaps his contemporaries found "The Way of Opinion" baffling and inconsistent with "The Way of

Truth," and that is why so little of it has survived. Theophrastus, a student of Aristotle, describes it as ". . . an account, in accordance with popular opinion, of the coming into being of sensible things."[13] However, G. S. Kirk and J. E. Raven propose that Parmenides is pointing out and then going on to describe a fundamental difference between Reality, What Is, which is perceived by reason, and appearances, which are perceived by the senses: whereas What Is cannot have an opposite (What Is Not cannot exist), what is perceived by the senses must be made up of opposites. Thus what is bright cannot be perceived by the senses except in contrast to dark.[14] In the fragmentary opening of "The Way of Opinion," he defines one pair of opposites, light (*phôs*) and darkness (*nùx*): "And when all things have been named light and night, and things corresponding to their powers have been assigned to each, everything is full of light and of obscure night at once, both equal, since neither has any share of nothingness."[15]

It is easy to see how Parmenides could use light and darkness to explain "in accordance with popular opinion" the appearance of the sun, moon, and other celestial bodies. It is not at all clear how he might have used them to explain the reproductive process in animals and humans (or its appearance). It seems likely, therefore, that he defined other sets of opposites to explain the perceptions of the other senses, for example heavy versus light, loud versus soft, cold versus hot, bitter versus sweet, pungent versus fragrant, and in the case of reproduction, possibly male versus female. If this is the case, it is too bad so little of "The Way of Opinion" has survived. It represents an interesting theory, which might have influenced the atomist theory of sensory perceptions.

Up to now, both the Milesians and Heraclitus taught that the archê, whatever they claimed it was, was a single element, from which all matter in its various forms was derived. Parmenides too, although he seems not to have speculated on the physical makeup of Reality, perceived it as one universal substance throughout. This belief that everything is formed out of one substance is called monism, from the Greek *monos,* "single, one."

However, some philosophers began to wonder whether there could be more than one source of matter, whether the universe was made up of multiple elements. Because they taught that there was more than one basic material, they are known as the pluralists, from the Latin *plures,* "more (than one)."

The most influential of the pluralists, in terms of his impact on later centuries, was the Sicilian Empedocles of Acragas, who lived from about 490 B.C. to about 430 B.C. Empedocles proposed the theory of the four "roots" (*rhizomata*) or elements: earth, water, air, and fire. On these, he said, two forces operated, Love, which mingled element with element, and Strife, which drove the elements apart. As Simplicius explains: "He [Empedocles] makes the material elements four in number, fire, air, water, and earth, all eternal but changing in bulk and scarcity through mixture and separation; but his real first principles, which impart motion to these, are Love and Strife. The elements are continually subject to an alternate change, at one time mixed together by Love, at another separated by Strife."[16]

All things that people perceive as coming into being or passing away are merely combinations of the four elements in various proportions, operated upon by Love and Strife. The elements themselves are indestructible and unchanging.

Empedocles' theory of the four elements was accepted by Aristotle, who became the source of all scientific knowledge in the Middle Ages, and the four elements became the

Empedocles (c. 490–430 B.C.) believed the universe was composed of various basic substances. He theorized that all matter could be reduced to the four elements of earth, fire, air, and water.

**The four elements as proposed by Empedocles: (clockwise from the top) fire, air, earth, and water.**

foundation of medieval and renaissance philosophy, science, and medicine, as well as astrology and alchemy. The belief in the four elements continued until it was eroded by modern scientific inquiry in the A.D. 1600s and 1700s (the Age of Reason).

Anaxagoras of Clazomenae, the philosopher who allegedly refused to let Democritus visit him in Athens, took Empedocles' theory of elements a step further. What Anaxagoras taught was very close to the atomic theory proposed by Leucippus and Democritus. He claimed, like Empedocles, that there is no such thing, really, as coming to be or passing away. All things that appear to come into being or degenerate are merely mixtures of elements coalescing or dissolving. Anaxagoras, however, did not propose a theory of four elements. Rather, he postulated a vast number of what he called "seeds" (*spérmata*), which come together to form all that can be perceived. These seeds were not only particles of materials, such as gold and water and flesh and hair. There were also particles of qualities, such as colors, tastes, heat, cold, hardness, and softness. Furthermore, all things contain seeds of every sort in some proportion. The appearance of something is determined by the sort of seeds it contains the most of. For example, blood contains seeds of blood, but also seeds of red, heat, and liquidity in the greatest proportion, but since blood can harden into a scab, it must also contain seeds of black, cold, and dryness. As Aristotle explains about the theory of Anaxagoras,

> The theory of Anaxagoras that the principles [seeds] are infinite in number was probably due to his acceptance of the common opinion of the physicists [pre-Socratics] that nothing comes into being from not-being. . . . Moreover, the fact that the opposites proceed from each other led them to the same conclusion. The one, they reasoned, must have already existed in the other; for since everything that comes into being must arise either from what is or from what is not, and it is impossible for it to arise from what is not (on this point all the physicists agree), they thought that the truth of the alternative necessarily followed, namely that things come into being out of existent things, *i.e.* out of things already present, but imperceptible to our senses because of the smallness of their

bulk. So they assert that everything is mixed in everything, because they saw everything arising out of everything. But things, as they say, appear different from one another and receive different names according to the nature of the thing that is numerically predominant among the innumerable constituents of the mixture. For nothing, they say, is purely and entirely white or black or sweet, or flesh or bones, but the nature of a thing is held to be that of which it contains the most.[17]

One passage in Simplicius, however, seems to suggest that there were not seeds of particular qualities, but that the seeds themselves contained various qualities, or perhaps all qualities in different proportions. For, says Simplicius, "we must suppose that there are many things of all sorts in everything . . . , seeds of all things with all sorts of shapes and colours and tastes."[18] Perhaps this is where the idea of "seeds within seeds" originated. Unfortunately, the fragments of Anaxagoras are so overexplained by later commentators who did not understand them very well (Aristotle included) that it is difficult to determine clearly from them what Anaxagoras's actual theories involved.

Anaxagoras attributes the cosmos, and everything in it, to the operation of a supreme intelligence upon the seeds, which he calls Mind (*Noûs*). This Mind is not mixed with the seeds; it is, says Simplicius, "infinite and self-ruled, and is mixed with nothing but is all alone by itself. . . . For it is the finest of all things and the purest, it has all knowledge about everything and the greatest power; and mind controls all things, both the greater and the smaller, that have life."[19] Mind created the universe by setting in motion a great rotation of everything (the seeds), and, says Simplicius, "as these things rotated thus [they] were separated off by the force and speed (of their rotation)."[20] In the course of the rotation, like things separated out and became the parts of the universe that can be perceived. It appears from what Simplicius says above about

Mind controlling all things that have life, that the presence or control of Mind in a being is what causes it to be alive.

From Anaxagoras's concept of seeds, it is not much of a leap to the theories of the first atomists, Leucippus and Democritus of Abdera, although there were significant differences between the two schools of thought. Atomism may also have been a response to the teachings of Parmenides, both a reaction to his theory that Reality is unchanging and unmoving, and an acceptance of his claim that Reality cannot be perceived by the senses.

# THE FIRST ATOMIC THEORY

THE FIRST THEORY INVOLVING ATOMS AS the primal stuff of matter is believed to have been developed by Leucippus of Abdera. Very little is known about Leucippus's life. He was probably not a native of Abdera, although he did most of his teaching there. He may have been a student of the Eleatic philosophers, a school that grew up in Elea, a city in southern Italy. In his early life he may have been a student of Zeno of Elea, who taught that matter and distance are capable of being infinitely divided, and used this theory to propose a number of confusing paradoxes, statements that contradict common experience. For example, Zeno argued that it was impossible to cross any distance, because the person must first cross half the distance, and then half of the remaining distance, and then half of that remaining distance, and so on forever. His conclusion was that all motion was impossible, a mere illusion. Here he was clearly drawing on the teachings of Parmenides. Leucippus must have decided that this sort of argument was nonsense, and proposed very small units of matter that cannot be divided further. He called these units *atomoi* ("incapable of being cut, indivisible"), or atoms. Aristotle explains, "Leucippus, however, thought he had a theory which harmonized with sense-perception and would not abolish either coming-to-be and passing-away or motion and the multiplicity of things. . . . What 'is' in the strict sense of the term is an absolute plenum [fullness, solidness]. This plenum, however, is not 'one': on the contrary, it is a 'many' infinite in number and invisible owing to the minuteness [smallness] of their bulk."[1]

Leucippus made one other vital contribution to scientific knowledge. While earlier philosophers, particularly the Eleatic school founded by

Parmenides, taught that nothingness, or "not being," could not exist, Leucippus taught that the universe consisted of atoms and void (*tò mè òn*, "the not being"), or vacuum, and that both were necessary for any form of matter to come into being: "He held that not-being exists as well as being, and the two are equally the causes of things coming-into-being. The nature of atoms he supposed to be compact and full; that, he said, was being, and it moved in the void, which he called not-being and held to exist no less than being."[2]

The other important idea that Leucippus may have introduced is that the number of atoms and the extent of the void are infinite, and that worlds are formed whenever large numbers of atoms develop a whirling motion that becomes a vortex, drawing the atoms together: "He also says . . . that the worlds are produced in this manner: That many bodies, of various kinds and shapes, are borne by amputation from the infinite, into a vast vacuum; and then, they being collected together, produce one vortex;

according to which they, dashing against one another, and whirling about in every direction, are separated in such a way that like attaches itself to like."[3]

Leucippus may have also developed the theory that the formation of worlds is random, and not the result of any conscious design. This idea, however, may have been arrived at by Democritus. Hippolytus of Rome, a Christian writer who lived in the A.D. 200s, has this to say about the atomists' theory of the random formation of worlds: "There are innumerable worlds, which differ in size. In some worlds there is no sun and moon, in others they are larger than in our world, and in others more numerous. The intervals between the worlds are unequal; in some parts there are more worlds, in others fewer; some are increasing, some at their height, some decreasing; in some parts they are arising, in others failing. They are destroyed by collision one with another. There are some worlds devoid of living creatures or plants or any moisture."[4]

The one fact that is fairly certain about Leucippus is that he settled in Abdera in Thrace,

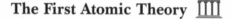

A seventeenth-century representation of the universe according to Democritus. The earth and planets are in the center surrounded by the stars in the heavens. The outermost circle is an infinite chaos of atoms, material from which worlds are randomly formed.

where he became the teacher of Democritus. Democritus adopted his teacher's theories, and systematized them and expanded them with ideas of his own.

Atoms, Democritus said, are not only indivisible but also unchangeable and eternal. They do not fuse together, but are constantly in motion, bouncing off one another and separated from one another by some degree of void. Although atoms are constantly bouncing off one another, some atoms form temporary bonds because they have tiny hooks or shapes that attract and attach them to other atoms. "As they [the atoms] move they collide and become entangled in such a way as to cling in close contact to one another. . . . The reason he gives for atoms staying together for a while is the intertwining and mutual hold of the primary bodies; for some of them are angular, some hooked, some concave, some convex, and indeed with countless other differences; so he thinks they cling to each other and stay together until such time as some stronger necessity [force] comes from the surrounding and shakes and scatters them apart."[5]

Various substances are made up of either one kind of atom (what we call elements, like gold or oxygen) or more than one kind of atom (what we call compounds, like salt or water).

The properties of any substance are determined by the shape, order (arrangement), and position (which way they face) of the atoms that compose it. Democritus compared the relationship of atoms in a substance to the letters of the alphabet: "These differences, they say, are three—shape and order and position. For they say the real is differentiated only by 'rhythm' and 'inter-contact' and 'turning'; and of these rhythm is shape, inter-contact is order, and turning is position; for A differs from N in shape, AN from NA in order, M from W in position."[6]

The shape, order, and position of atoms in a compound help units of a compound to bond together with other units of the same sort, and eventually form masses that are visible to humans. "These atoms move in the infinite void, separate one from the other and differing in shapes, sizes, position, and arrangement; overtaking each other they collide, and some are shaken away in any chance direction, while others, becoming intertwined one with another according to the congruity of their shapes, sizes, positions, and arrangements, stay together and so effect the coming into being of compound bodies."[7]

The shape of a substance's atoms and the amount of void between them determine its properties: hard, soft, dense, fragile, liquid, solid, and so forth. Air and fire, for example, are made up of smooth, widely separated atoms; gold is made of closely bonded atoms that are resistant to coming apart. There is some question about whether Democritus believed atoms had weight. Aristotle thinks he did: "And yet Democritus says 'the more any indivisible [atom] exceeds [in size], the heavier it is.'"[8] However, Aetius, a late (around 100 B.C.) writer of a history of philosophy, says otherwise:

> Democritus named two (properties of atoms), size and shape.[9]
>
> Democritus says that the primary bodies [atoms] do not possess weight but move in the infinite [void] as the result of striking one another.[10]

Some of the fragments of Democritus's writings seem to make a case for weight being a factor of how much atomic material versus how much void a substance contains. Substances with closely compacted atoms and less void were heavier, while substances with loosely connected atoms and more void were lighter. As Theophrastus writes, "In compound bodies [bodies in which atoms have come together] the lighter is that which contains more void, the heavier that which contains less."[11] But even in that case, atoms would still have to have weight, if substances with more compacted atoms are heavier, and substances with atoms more separated by void are lighter. Perhaps Democritus dealt with this problem in a text that no longer survives.

Both Leucippus and Democritus rejected the existence of gods, or any sort of divine influence in creation and dissolution. They taught that the formation and dissolution of all things is due to necessity (natural laws dependent on the properties of atoms) and chance (the random

45

coming together and breaking apart of atoms). "(On the nature of necessity) Democritus means by it the resistance and movement and blows of matter [that is, the atoms]."[12]

Human perception of the world depends on both the coming together of the right sorts of atoms to form masses large enough to be seen or felt, and the constant sloughing off of atoms from these masses.

# 4

# HOW HUMANS
# PERCEIVE THE
# WORLD

IF THE UNIVERSE CONSISTS OF NOTHING but atoms bouncing off one another and occasionally coalescing into elements or compounds, all whirling about in the vortex, why do humans perceive the world as they do? For it is clear that the world looks nothing at all the way Democritus perceived it. Leucippus and Democritus pondered the question, and came up with a theory: Living things that grow and live on the worlds formed out of the whirling vortexes have organs that allow them to perceive the world around them. They have sight and smell and taste and hearing and touch, and therefore they can, in a limited and mostly mistaken way, gain an idea of the world around them.

Vision, for example, is the result of layers of atoms peeling off the objects around them, and moving through the air until they strike the eye of a living thing. Democritus called these membranes *eidola*, "images." As described by Alexander of Aphrodisias, a commentator on Aristotle writing in the late A.D. 200s, "They attributed sight to certain images, of the same shape as the object, which were continually streaming off from the objects of sight and impinging on the eye."[1]

These images shrink as they move through the air, so that the eye perceives something far away as small, and something closer as nearer to its actual size. The constant sloughing of images accounted, they said, for the deterioration of physical objects over time.

Democritus's theory of color is rather confusing. This may be due to Theophrastus's description of it, for it seems to have confused Theophrastus. Theophrastus says that Democritus defined four primary colors: white, black, red, and greenish-yellow (*chlôros*). (The Greeks did not classify colors quite the way we do. The color *chlôros* ran the gamut from emerald green to the yellow of egg yolks. Likewise the poet Homer describes a dark blue sea as "wine-dark," apparently lumping together very dark blue, purple, and dark wine red. The famous Tyrian "purple" used to dye the robes of kings and the senatorial stripes of the Romans was what we would describe as a deep crimson red.)

Things that appeared white are made up of smooth atoms separated by straight openings to let light through. Things that appear black consist of rough, uneven atoms that are not aligned to let light through. Red is made of smooth atoms like fire, only larger. Things that merely become red contain these larger atoms, but things that burst into flame contain the smaller, more volatile fire atoms. Greenish-yellow consists of a mixture of atoms and void, varying according to the arrangement of the atoms.

All other colors are the result of mixing atoms that reflect the primary colors; for example, dark blue consists of black and greenish-yellow.[2]

What is known about Democritus's theory of sound and hearing is sketchy, but what little there is seems surprisingly accurate. He had no concept of sound waves, of course, but says that "the air is broken up into bodies of like shape and is rolled along together with fragments of the voice."[3] These bodies, striking the ear, result in hearing: "Sound occurs when the air is condensed and penetrates with force."[4]

Democritus was quite explicit about taste, which is caused by substances composed of certain kinds of atoms coming in contact with the tongue. For example, foods with a sharp flavor consist of small, fine-grained atoms with a zigzag shape. (What he seems to mean by this is hot or pungent foods, like raw garlic, since he describes them as "heating" the body.) Sweet foods like honey consist of medium-sized round atoms that "flow through and permeate the entire body, but not violently or quickly." Sour foods consist of large angular atoms that cause the veins to constrict and pucker up. Bitter substances are made up of small, round atoms with spikes on them. Salty foods contain large, often irregular, rough atoms; their size caused them to rise to the top instead of being mixed with all the other atoms, which is why salty foods mostly taste salty.[5]

Democritus's theories on the sense of smell and the sense of touch have not survived.

One point upon which Democritus was very firm was that living beings do not perceive the world as it really is. Human perception is determined by the interaction of atoms and sense organs. (Democritus is almost right. What we perceive as red, for example, is the color of the light that is *reflected* from the object. What the human eye perceives is a sort of photo *negative* of what is really out there. If we could see the actual object, it would be a shade of vivid turquoise.) Because human sense organs generally perceive the same combination of atoms in the same way, people arrive at certain conventions for describing the world around them. For example, a poppy is "red," honey is "sweet," the air disturbed by the braying of a donkey strikes the ear as both "loud" and "discordant." But in fact the physical world contains none of these qualities. What humans perceive as the qualities of the physical world are unreal. There is really no such thing as color, sweetness, bitterness, loudness, softness, odor, roughness, or smoothness. There is only the effect of atoms making an impact on human sense organs, which are themselves only collections of atoms, as we know today they are.

As Democritus says, "By convention are sweet and bitter, hot and cold, by convention is colour; in truth are atoms and the void. . . . In reality we apprehend nothing exactly, but only as it changes according to the condition of our body and of the things that impinge on or offer resistance to it."[6]

Democritus sums up by saying, "There are two forms of knowledge, one genuine, one obscure. To the obscure belong all the following: sight, hearing, smell, taste, touch. The other is genuine, and is quite distinct from this."[7]

This argument of Democritus seems to have

been influenced by the teachings of Parmenides. "Genuine" knowledge is intellectual, the knowledge of the mind. It accepts the information coming in from the senses, uses it to form conceptions of the physical world, and then proceeds further, trying to understand what is really out there, what the physical world is really made of. Only intellectually can humans conceive of atoms and the void, which is the reality hidden from them by the imperfect perceptions of the senses.

The mind, said Democritus, is the same as the soul, which is the thing that separates the living being from the inanimate one. For only living things are infused with some substance that enables them to move about and gives them understanding.[8]

# 5

# THE NATURE OF LIVING THINGS

ACCORDING TO DEMOCRITUS, LIVING things—animals and human beings—are no different from stones and earth and water and air and all the other things that make up the universe in that they too are formed from the coming together of atoms. Their creation depends just as much on necessity and chance as that of anything else in the world, and there is nothing divinely inspired about their coming into being. Living things are different in just one important respect—they are infused with something he called *psychê,* or soul.

"Life" was a difficult concept for the Greek philosophers. What *did* set living things apart from things that were not alive? The philosophers argued long and hard about what made living things live.

In pre-philosophical ages, people thought of psychê as what made the body alive,[1] and they associated it with breath.[2] After all, when a living thing stopped breathing, the body was still there, but it was not alive. It is not surprising, therefore, to find Anaximenes associating the soul with breath or air, and explaining that it holds the body together in the same way that his archê, air, holds the universe together.[3] As soon as the breath departs, the body begins to break down.

Heraclitus likewise identified the soul with his archê, in this case fire. Just as fire is put out with water, so the soul dies when it becomes too wet (that is, living things die if they drown).[4] Heraclitus seems also to have identified the soul with intelligence. He points out that when someone becomes drunk (that is, dampens his soul), both his intelligence and his strength deteriorate. Heraclitus observes that "a dry soul is wisest and best," implying that drinking wine is not a good idea.[5]

Democritus denied that the soul had any supernatural qualities. Like Heraclitus, he believed that it was made up of fire, but he also believed that fire was no more divine than any other type of atom, and certainly was not any sort of archê. He argued that atoms of fire were the smallest and most mobile of the atoms, spherical and constantly in motion. He equated fire with mind—that is, thought and intelligence— The same atoms in a living thing are called "soul" and in an inanimate thing "fire." Thus their presence does not distinguish an animate form from an inanimate matter. "Democritus has expressed himself more ingeniously than the rest," Aristotle said, "on the grounds for ascribing each of these two characters to soul; soul and mind are, he says, one and the same thing, and this thing must be one of the primary and indivisible bodies, and its power of originating movement must be due to its fineness of grain and the shape of its atoms; he says that of all the shapes the spherical is the most mobile, and that this is the shape of the particles of fire and mind."[6]

These tiny, spherical atoms are what give living things the power of motion, one of the things that sets them apart from inanimate objects. Being so small and mobile, these soul atoms permeate every part of the body and give animals and humans the power to move about: "Some say that what originates movement is both pre-eminently and primarily soul; believing that what is not itself moved cannot originate movement in another, they arrived at the view that soul belongs to the class of things in movement. This is what led Democritus to say that soul is a sort of fire or hot substance; his 'forms' or atoms are infinite in number; those which are spherical he calls fire and soul, . . . This implies the view that soul is identical with what produces movement in animals."[7]

Democritus also works breath into the stuff of life, for he argues that living things breathe in "soul" atoms from the atmosphere, which contains some fire atoms. In this way, they acquire more life, soul, and mind by breathing: "That is why, further, they regard respiration as the characteristic mark of life; as the environment compresses the bodies of animals, and tends to extrude those atoms which impart movement to them, because they themselves are never at rest, there must be a reinforcement of these by similar atoms coming in from without in the act of respiration."[8]

These atoms are not specifically fire or soul, but merely the smallest and most mobile of atoms. Their nature depends on their surroundings. In a living being, they are soul/mind; in a pile of dead wood, given the right encouragement, they are fire.[9]

Another characteristic of living things that inanimate objects do not share is the ability to reproduce. Democritus's theory of how this happens is one of those cases where he is amazingly close to the truth. He believed that human and animal reproduction is the result of "seeds" (we would call them sperm and ova) produced by the male and the female, each of which contained material from every part of the parent's body (we would call these chromosomes or genes).[10] The sex of the offspring was determined by whichever seed contained more material from the parent's genitals. "Democritus of Abdera also says that the differentiation of sex takes place within the mother; . . . it depends on the question which parent it is whose semen prevails,—not the whole of the semen, but that which has come from the part by which male and female differ from one another."[11]

Democritus does not say anything about the nature of plants. He may have done so in writings that have not survived, or he may not have regarded plants as living things equivalent to humans and animals.

Besides exploring how humans and animals reproduce, Democritus explored the theory of how animals and humans come to live together with their own kind, and the development of human societies.

# 6

# THE EVOLUTION OF HUMAN SOCIETY

AS MIGHT BE EXPECTED, THE ATOMISTS disagreed with Greek mythology on how human societies came into being.

As recorded by Hesiod in his poem *Works and Days,* the human race was created by the gods in stages as a sort of experiment. First they created a golden race, who lived virtuously in abundance of all good things and suffered no sickness or old age but died as if falling asleep. After the golden race had passed from the earth, the gods created a silver race, less noble than the golden race, who sinned against one another and did not honor the gods. So the gods destroyed them and brought forth a race of bronze, far worse than the silver race, who waged war and destroyed one another until the whole race was wiped out. After that, the gods brought forth a race of heroes, the great kings and warriors of the Greek epics. And last of all, the gods brought forth the race of iron, which is the race that now inhabits the earth, who "never rest from labor and

The first page of Hesiod's *Work and Days*. The original Greek text is on the left and a Latin translation is on the right.

sorrow" and will sin until society breaks down and the gods destroy them.[1]

(It has been suggested that the myth of the five ages is some kind of race memory. The gold and silver ages are the development of human civilization, from the relatively carefree days of stone-age hunting and gathering, down through the beginnings of agriculture and village life in the Neolithic. Then the bronze age (1800–1600 B.C.), saw the emergence of Greek civilization in the Mycenaean period (1600–1100 B.C., the age of heroes in which the Trojan War was fought). The so-called dark (iron) age followed the invasion of Greece by the iron-wielding Dorians (1100–750 B.C.), which destroyed the Mycenaean civilization.)

Democritus preferred to trust to his own observations on how animals and humans come together. No fragments survive from Democritus himself about the evolution of human society, but a reasonable reconstruction can be made from the epic poem *On the Nature of the Universe*[2] by the Roman poet Lucretius (c. 99–49 B.C.). His epic is a celebration of the philosophical teachings of the philosopher Epicurus (341–270 B.C.), who in turn based his Epicurean philosophy on the teachings of Democritus. Lucretius may have based his poem not only on the texts of Epicurus, but on the writings of Democritus as well. If he did not have access to the original texts of Democritus, he could have had at least a commentary by some later editor.[3]

What Lucretius drew from Democritus and Epicurus has an eerie resemblance to what modern scientists tell us about the evolution of humanity. Democritus had, after all, traveled most of the known world in his youth, and he had probably seen societies in all stages of development. He knew sophisticated Greeks and Persians, and he may have seen people still using stone weapons. This sort of culture was not unknown in antiquity. The historian Herodotus (484–425 B.C.), roughly contemporaneous with Democritus and also a world traveler, mentions "Ethiopians" fighting in the army of the Persian King Xerxes, clad in lion and leopard skins and armed with bows and stone-tipped arrows.[4]

Lucretius (c. 99–49 B.C.), the Roman poet and philosopher who composed *On the Nature of the Universe*, an epic poem based on the teachings of Epicurus and Democritus.

Democritus may have been in a position to write with some authority about how primitive people lived, as well as people in more civilized ways of life. He was also able to explore backwards to what the most primitive humans must have been like. Lucretius's description of earliest man agrees closely with the evidence archaeologists have discovered about the physical appearance of both the Neanderthals and the ancestral *homo sapiens* population that departed Africa some fifty thousand years ago to populate the world[5]: "The *human beings* that peopled these fields were far tougher than the men of to-day, as became the offspring of tough earth. They were built on a framework of bigger and solider bones, fastened through their flesh to stout sinews. They were relatively insensitive to heat and cold, to unaccustomed diet and bodily ailments in general."[6] He describes quite accurately the habits of a hunting-gathering society: "They lived out their lives in the fashion of wild beasts roaming at large. . . . Their hearts were well content to accept as a free gift what the sun and showers had given and the earth had produced unsolicited. Often they stayed their hunger among the acorn-laden oaks. Arbutus berries, whose scarlet tint now betrays their winter ripening, were then produced by the earth in plenty and of a larger size. In addition the lusty childhood of the earth yielded a great variety of tough foods, ample for afflicted mortals."[7]

Lucretius describes cave dwellers who hunted wild beasts for food: "They lived in thickets and hillside caves and forests, . . . Thanks to their surpassing strength of hand and foot, they hunted the woodland beasts by hurling stones and wielding ponderous clubs. They were more than a match for many of them; from a few they took refuge in hiding-places."[8]

He also derived from Democritus and Epicurus a description of the first human civilization: the building of huts (compare the homes built from mammoth bones by eastern European stone-age hunters[9]), the wearing of clothes, the use of fire, and the beginnings of social institutions: "As time went by, men began to build huts and use skins and fire. Men and women learnt to live together in a stable union and to watch over their [children]. Then it was that that humanity first began to mellow."[10]

Soon after this, says Lucretius, families began to bond together into tribal societies, and social customs and laws were established. (Scientists

An illustration of Neanderthals cutting up the beast they just killed. Democritus's thoughts on the evolution of human society were remarkably similar to modern-day views.

today think that these probably centered at first around cooperative hunting and gathering and the fair division of food.) "Then neighbors began to form mutual alliances, wishing neither to do nor to suffer violence among themselves."[11]

Humans learned to express themselves in speech: "As for the various sounds of *spoken language,* it was nature that drove men to utter these, and practical convenience that gave a form to the names of objects. . . . And what, after all, was so surprising in the notion that the human race, possessed of a vigorous voice and tongue, should indicate objects by various vocal utterances expressive of various feelings?"[12]

Humans also learned to make fire and to cook their food. In this way they gained the advantages that heating could contribute to their diet. (It is interesting that Michael Pallen, in *The Omnivore's Dilemma,* attributes the growth of the human brain to, among other things, the complexities of cooking foods that would have been inedible or even poisonous if they had been eaten raw.[13]) "Later it was the sun that taught them to cook food and soften it by heating on the flames, since they noticed in roaming through the fields how many things were subdued and mellowed by the impact of its ardent rays."[14]

Then, says Lucretius, it was not long until headmen became kings, and people began to build cities, herd cattle, and grow crops. After that came gold and a money economy, and, says Lucretius in the true Roman fashion, it was all downhill from there until the common people, disgusted at the way things were going, learned to decree laws and frame constitutions. But by then humanity was well on its way to settled government and written history.

It is surprising that Democritus's scientific theories had so small an impact on people in Greek and Roman times. Those who accepted them were interested in them mainly as a basis on which to found a philosophy for living in interesting and very troubled times.

# 7

# DEMOCRITUS'S IMPACT ON THE ANCIENT WORLD

THE ANCIENT WORLD OF THE GREEKS and the Romans was not particularly interested in Democritus's theory of atoms. What they related to was the system of ethics he developed based on his atomic theory.

Democritus gave a great deal of thought to what a godless world of random atoms bouncing off one another, sometimes connecting, sometimes being drawn into a vortex that formed a cosmos, meant for the intelligent human creatures that emerged out of this atomic free-for-all.

Democritus rejected the theory of gods assigning laws to mortals. He saw human beings as being responsible for determining moral actions for themselves because it was the only way to live peacefully with one another, without fear of retaliation or judgment of their fellow men. He argued that the person who behaved justly and honorably could live at peace with himself: "The cheerful man, who is eager for just and lawful deeds, rejoices whether waking or sleeping and is strong and free from care; but he that cares nought for justice and does not the things that are right finds all such things joyless, when he remembers them, and is afraid and reproaches himself."[1]

Nor can wealth make a person happy. The soul (which Democritus identified with the mind) is the dwelling place of happiness or misery. A poor man who behaves justly to other people is happy, while a man rich in gold and cattle who has wronged his fellow men lives in fear and self-reproach, because he lives with the ill will of those around him.

Speaking from experience as a world traveler, Democritus says that when one's basic needs are met, one can be content: "Service abroad teaches self sufficiency; barley-bread and a straw mattress are the pleasantest medicines for hunger and fatigue."[2]

Anyone who has traveled across Europe or explored places like Nepal or Indonesia with a backpack and not a lot of cash knows the truth of this. Travel is broadening. Traveling with minimal baggage teaches one to live minimally and relish everything that new places and new experiences have to offer.

What Democritus promoted then was "restraint, common sense, and sanity."[3] He believed that happiness was to be found in the soul, not in external wealth or property or power, or even the strength and beauty of the body. Not that these external things are bad; but they are good only to the extent of what the soul makes of them. Use them badly, and they become bad. Use beauty or strength or wealth to harm others, and they become destructive, and ruin the soul as well. Use them well, virtuously, and they are good, both for the soul and for one's fellows.

However, one must learn understanding, to know how best to use one's assets. Reason and wisdom and self-discipline must be learned, if a person is to achieve happiness: "Education is an adornment in good fortune and a refuge in misfortune."[4]

If one leaves one's life to chance, one is bound to be out of control, at the mercy of whatever life brings. But the person who learns reason and self-control can achieve a measure of cheerfulness, serenity, and contentment, whatever is happening in the external world.

Above all, Democritus taught that people should not fear death, for there is no afterlife full of torments and punishments. Death is simply a dissolution, one's atoms returning to the universe, to be formed again into some other being. People fear death because they believe in punishment in an afterlife: "Some people, ignorant of the dissolution of mortal nature, but conscious of their evil-doing in life, trouble their time of life with terrors and fears, inventing false tales about the time after death."[5]

But, said Democritus, there is no afterlife. The soul is mortal as well as the body. Therefore there is nothing to fear from death, which is indeed often an end of suffering.

Democritus's vigorous philosophy appealed to Greeks in later centuries, when they had lost their freedom to govern themselves, first to Philip of Macedon and his son Alexander the Great, and later to the Romans. Deprived of self-determination, governed by officials at best corrupt, at worst insane, they developed philosophies that would enable one to survive and maintain one's self-respect in a world that seemed to have gone mad. These philosophies were Stoicism, founded by Zeno of Citium (334–262 B.C.), and Epicureanism, taught by Epicurus. Epicurus adopted Democritus's theory of atomic materialism (atheism, the mortal soul, and the absence of an afterlife) and taught that the best life was to seek modest pleasures, and by exercising reason and self-control to achieve a state of mind he called *ataraxia,* that is, tranquility and peace of mind. The Epicurean

A bust of Epicurus (341–270 B.C.). Epicurean philosophy emphasized prudence, moderation, and friendship. It also taught that there were no gods or an afterlife, and therefore, people should not live in fear of death or fret about things that were out of their control.

way of life consisted mostly of keeping one's head down, not calling attention to oneself by acquiring great wealth or power, and practicing moderation and virtue. Epicurus set great value on friendship and the enjoyment of pleasure, which he defined as the absence of pain. His school in Athens was called the Garden, and his students, which included women, practiced a discipline marked by simplicity and self-control.

Epicureanism attracted some Romans, including the poets Lucretius and Horace. It disappeared during the Middle Ages, when pagan philosophies were suppressed by the Christian Church. It revived during the Renaissance (A.D. 1300–1600) and the Age of Reason (A.D. 1600–1800), and attracted, among other eminent intellectuals, Thomas Jefferson, which is how "the pursuit of happiness" got into the Declaration of Independence.

It is ironic, given the austere way of life cultivated by Epicurus and his followers, that in later times "epicurean" came to mean a way of life devoted to sensual enjoyment, especially luxurious and excessive eating and drinking. The Yiddish word for a Jew who does not observe religious practices, especially kosher dietary laws, is *apikoros*.[6] The word comes from the name of Epicurus, who would not have understood the association with his teachings at all.

# 8

# THE IMPACT OF DEMOCRITUS ON MODERN SCIENCE

IF THE SCIENCE OF THE ATOMISTS Leucippus and Democritus had a minor impact on the ancient world except as a springboard to ethical philosophy, it had a remarkable effect on the modern age of science, which started in the late 1700s and shows no sign of stopping yet. What is amazing to modern researchers is how often Democritus was right, or almost right. He was perfectly correct about atoms and vacuum, and atoms bouncing about in the vacuum, hitting one another and bouncing off. He was wrong about fire being an element; he had no concept of the difference between matter and energy, and concluded that after all, a person could see and touch an element, and could also see fire, and feel it too by sticking a finger in it, so fire must be an element. In the same way, he did not understand that light was energy, and waves of light, bouncing off objects in the physical world, were received by the eye so that an object could be seen. Of course he was wrong about atoms being the smallest unit of matter and being impossible to split, but then so were quite a few modern explorers into the technicalities of atomic theory. After all, Democritus did not have the advantages of modern technology for exploring the world of subatomic particles.

Democritus was also correct that atoms combined to form elements and compounds, though they do not do so in quite the way he envisioned. The link between Democritus's atomic theory and modern chemistry began with the idea of elements—substances composed of only one sort of atom. This concept was introduced by Antoine Lavoisier (1743–1794), a French chemist. Lavoisier first discovered that there were certain materials that, unlike compounds like water and salt, could not be reduced to any simpler substance by any method of chemical analysis. He

French chemist Antoine Lavoisier (1743–1794), the founder of modern chemistry.

called these substances elements, and catalogued them into what is recognized as the first example of a periodic table.

Another French chemist, Joseph Louis Proust (1754–1826), discovered the Law of Definite Proportions, which states that a chemical compound always contains the same proportion of elements, determined by mass.

However, the real father of modern atomic theory was an Englishman named John Dalton (1766–1844). Dalton found that he could explain the properties of the gases that made up the air by referring to the studies of the atom by Democritus. Dalton concluded that atoms, which he named from Democritus's *atomoi*, were

**English chemist John Dalton (1766–1844), the father of modern atomic theory.**

the stuff that made up elements, substances made of a single type of atom. He also discovered that all atoms that make up a particular element are identical in the way they combine with other atoms in chemical reactions.

Dalton also determined that atoms could combine into compounds (substances made up of more than one kind of atom), the smallest unit of which he called a molecule. When molecules are subjected to a chemical process, the atoms are not destroyed, but are formed into new molecules.

Robert Brown (1773–1858), a botanist studying the way pollen grains behaved in water, observed when he placed a sample under a

# ATOMIC SYMBOLS

*John Dalton, D.C.L, F.R.S &c.&c.*

*explanatory of a*

## LECTURE

*given by him to the MEMBERS of the*

### Manchester Mechanics' Institution,

*October 19th 1835.*

John Dalton invented a system of symbols for chemical substances. The ones at the top represent the elements. Below them are the oxides (compounds containing oxygen) and sulphurets (or sulfides, compounds containing sulfur). The last group consists of other chemical compounds, which are arranged according to how many elements make them up. For example, *binary* means two, *ternary* means three, etc.

microscope that the pollen grains were in constant motion. Although he had no microscope powerful enough to see what was causing the motion, he concluded that the pollen grains were constantly being pelted by minute particles, from which they rebounded. In this case, the particles were water molecules. This sort of agitation is now called Brownian motion, after the man who discovered it.

Up to this time, however, scientists accepted Democritus's dictum that an atom was the smallest unit of matter, and could not be subdivided. Then in 1897, J. J. Thomson, the director of the Cavendish Laboratory at Cambridge University, discovered an electrically charged particle that was much smaller than an atom. His discovery, the electron, galvanized the world of physics and led a young colleague of his, Ernest Rutherford (1871–1937), to start exploring the structure of the atom. He used alpha particles, the positive nuclei of helium atoms, to bombard thin sheets of gold and silver, which are also elements. The results were

Physicist Ernest Rutherford (1871–1937), the father of nuclear science. One of his many contributions to nuclear physics was devising the nuclear model of the atom.

astonishing. Most of the time, the alpha particles passed through the sheets, but sometimes they bounced off at odd angles, or even rebounded. From this experiment Rutherford concluded that an atom is mostly made up of empty space, with a tiny nucleus carrying a positive electrical charge, orbited by negatively charged electrons. So much for Democritus's theory that atoms are solid and impenetrable!

Not long afterwards, it was discovered that the nucleus of the atom is made up of protons, particles with a positive charge, and neutrons, particles with no electrical charge. The nucleus was orbited by electrons with a negative charge.

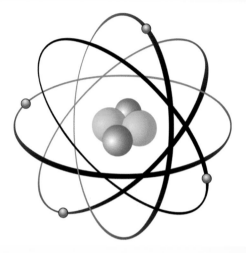

This atomic model shows the nucleus, which is made up of protons and neutrons, and the orbiting electrons.

The comparison to the solar system, with planets orbiting a central sun, was irresistible.

In the 1930's, Italian scientist Enrico Fermi began experiments of bombarding uranium with neutrons. In 1938, the German scientist Otto Hahn (1879–1968) continued these experiments, and was amazed to find lighter elements left behind as a result. The heavy uranium atoms had been split into lighter atoms, and enormous energy had been released in the process. (Albert Einstein had demonstrated this with his famous formula $E = mc^2$. The energy released from splitting an atom equals the difference between mass of the original atom and the mass of the

An illustration of nuclear (atomic) fission, the splitting of an atom.

atoms created by the split, multiplied by the speed of light squared).

Hahn was puzzled by what had happened. He contacted his friend and colleague Lise Meitner and her nephew Otto Frisch, who had taken refuge in Sweden to escape the Nazi persecution of the Jews. They realized that what Hahn had caused was a process they called atomic fission (splitting). As the uranium atoms were split by Hahn's barrage of neutrons, they released more neutrons, creating a chain reaction that could either be harnessed for controlled nuclear power (for example, in a nuclear reactor) or used to build an incredibly destructive atomic bomb.

The United States, fearing that Germany would learn how to apply this knowledge to

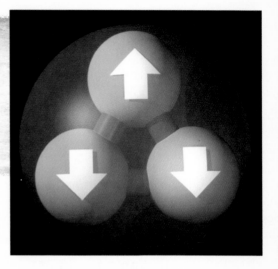

This shows the structure of a neutron, which consists of one up and two down quarks. The red structures are called gluons and hold the quarks together.

creating such an atomic bomb, initiated the Manhattan Project to develop its own atomic arsenal. In 1945 the first two atomic bombs were detonated, destroying the Japanese cities of Hiroshima and Nagasaki.

Since then, research has shown the atom to be made up of more particles than protons, neutrons, and electrons. After the war, scientists were able to build powerful linear accelerators in which they could slam particles into atoms and study the new particles that were released. They had hoped to discover a clear picture of how atoms were formed. Instead, the list of subatomic particles kept expanding. Physicists discovered whole "families" of subatomic particles, and started trying to classify them as fermions, bosons, leptons, and hadrons.

Finally, Murray Gell-Mann and George Zweig determined that the behavior of these particles could be explained by identifying a smaller fundamental particle of which the hadrons were made up. Gell-Mann called this particle a quark. He first identified three different "flavors" of quarks, identified by their charge: up, down, and strange. Later experiments added additional flavors: charm, truth, and beauty. Quarks have fractional charges; in combination their charges add up to an integer. A proton, for example, is made up of two up and one down quark, whose charges adds up to a positive one. A neutron is made up of one up and two down quarks, whose charges add up to zero. The electron is a lepton, which like the quark is a fundamental building block, and so far has not been subdivided.

That is where the matter stands right now. Will physicists one day split the quark and the lepton and discover still smaller building blocks?

Or is it quarks and leptons all the way down? Democritus no doubt would be surprised at what modern science has found out about his atomoi. He would surely be pleased to discover how often he got it right.

 # ACTIVITIES

## Activity 1

**Materials:**

- ◈ beans in a couple of sizes and some lentils
- ◈ a large wire sieve
- ◈ an adult

**Procedure:**

1. Place the beans and lentils in the sieve.

2. Ask the adult who is helping you to shake the sieve in a circular motion so that the contents whirl around inside it. This is how Democritus described the model of his vortex.

3. When your helper has finished whirling the sieve, look to see if the beans and lentils have "flocked together" according to their different kinds. Was Democritus right when he said, "For creatures . . . flock together with their kind, doves with doves, cranes with cranes, and so on. And the same happens even with inanimate things, as can be seen with seeds in a sieve"?

# Activity 2

**Materials:**

◈ Ping-Pong balls in assorted colors (red, green, blue, yellow, white)

◈ a strip of Velcro tape about a foot long (the Velcro tape should contain both a strip with hooks and a strip with fuzz, stuck together)

◈ scissors

◈ glue

◈ a large, see-through plastic container with a snap-on lid, big enough that the Ping-Pong balls put inside it have plenty of room to move around

**Procedure:**

1. Cut the Velcro tape into pieces about ½ inch long.

2. Select Ping-Pong balls of two colors, say red and yellow.

3. For each Ping-Pong ball you have chosen, separate a square of Velcro tape into its hooked side and its fuzzy side.

4. Glue the hooked side of the square to one side of the Ping-Pong ball, and the fuzzy side of the square to the other side of the Ping-Pong ball so that the hooked

side and the fuzzy side are facing outward.

5.  Let the glue dry.

6.  Place all the Ping-Pong balls, both the ones with Velcro squares and the ones without, inside the plastic container. Snap the lid on.

7.  Shake the plastic container hard, both from side to side and up and down, so that the Ping-Pong balls fly around in all directions. This is a model of Democritus's description of atoms in the void flying around and bouncing off one another.

8.  Stop shaking the container. Remove the lid.

9.  Look to see if any of the Velcro-ed Ping-Pong balls have stuck together.

10. Remove any clusters of stuck-together balls and look at them. Balls of the same color that have stuck together are elements, made up of the same kind of atoms. Balls of different colors that have stuck together are molecules of compounds, made up of atoms of different kinds.

# CHRONOLOGY

**Note:** The abbreviation "c." from Latin "circa" means "about, approximately."

**c. 550 B.C.**—Beginning of the Milesian school of philosophy, at the city of Miletos in Asia Minor (now Turkey). Thales was the first of the Milesian philosophers. His followers included Anaximander and Anaximenes. They inquired into what the physical world was made of, and defined several kinds of archê, or primal material.

**c. 500 B.C.**—Heraclitus of Ephesus begins teaching. Heraclitus believed the archê was fire.

**c. 460 B.C.**—Democritus is born at Abdera, into a wealthy Abderite family.

**c. 450 B.C.**—Empedocles of Acragas introduces his theory of the four "roots" from which the universe was made up: earth, water, fire, and air. Empedocles was the first of the pluralists; Anaxagoras begins teaching his theory of "seeds" containing every sort of matter, controlled by Noûs, or Mind; Leucippus settles at Abdera. Sometime thereafter Democritus becomes his student.

**c. 440 B.C.**—Democritus travels to Athens to study philosophy and meet with Anaxagoras. He comes away disappointed, and returns to Abdera.

**c. 430 B.C.**—Democritus's father dies and leaves him a tidy fortune. Democritus sets out on his travels to Egypt, the Middle East, and India, returning by way of Ethiopia.

**c. 420 B.C.**—Democritus returns to Abdera and devotes the rest of his life to study, teaching, and writing.

**c. 370 B.C.**—Democritus dies at Abdera and is awarded a public funeral by his fellow citizens.

**c. 341B.C.**—Epicurus is born on the island of Samos. He becomes a follower of Democritus and converts his atomic theory into a philosophy of life.

**c. 270 B.C.**—Epicurus dies at Athens.

**c. 99 B.C.**—Lucretius (Titus Lucretius Carus) is born. Around 55 b.c. he begins to compose his great epic on the teachings of Epicurus, *On the Nature of the Universe*.

**c. 49 B.C.**—Lucretius dies at Rome.

**A.D. 380**—A long dry spell begins here for atomic theory. The Christian Church did not like Democritus and his followers because of their atheism, and vigorously suppressed their writings. Not much was heard of the atomists until the Age of Reason, over twelve hundred years later.

**1789**—Antoine Lavoisier publishes his *Treatise of Elementary Chemistry*, which defined an element as a substance that could not be broken down by any known chemical process and explained how compounds are formed from elements.

**1784–1785**—Robert Brown, a Scottish botanist, discovers and describes Brownian motion, establishing the existence of water molecules.

**1800**—John Dalton begins his explorations into atoms, elements, compounds, and molecules.

**1897**—J. J. Thomson discovers the electron.

**1907**—Ernest Rutherford and his assistants Hans Geiger (of Geiger counter fame) and Ernest Marsden define the nuclear structure of the atom.

**1934**—Enrico Fermi begins experimenting with uranium.

**1938**—Otto Hahn, Lise Meitner, and Otto Frisch identify the processes known as atomic fission and a neutron chain reaction.

**1945**—The United States drops the first two atomic bombs on the Japanese cities of Hiroshima and Nagasaki. So far, these have been the only nuclear bombs used in war.

**1964**—Murray Gell-Mann and George Zweig independently postulate the existence of the quark.

# CHAPTER NOTES

## Chapter 1. The Life and Times of Democritus

1. J. J. O'Connor and E. F. Robertson, "Democritus of Abdera," *The MacTutor History of Mathematics*, 1999, <http://www-history.mcs.st-andrews.ac.uk/Biographies/Democritus.html> (September 29, 2007).

2. Ibid.

3. Ibid.

4. Ibid.

5. Diogenes Laertius, "The Life of Democritus (section III)," *The Lives and Opinions of Eminent Philosophers*, Book IX, trans. C. D. Yonge, n.d., <http://www.classicpersuasion.org/pw/diogenes/index.htm> (November 13, 2007).

6. Ibid., section II.

7. Ibid.

8. Ibid.

9. *Stanford Encyclopedia of Philosophy*, s.v. "Democritus" (by Sylvia Berryman), <http://plato.stanford.edu/entries/democritus/> (September 10, 2007); G. S. Kirk and J. E. Raven, *The Presocratic Philosophers: A Critical History With a Selection of Texts* (Cambridge: Cambridge University Press, 1957), pp. 402–403.

10. Laertius, section VII.

## Chapter 2. What Is Matter Made Of?

1. Hesiod *Theogony* lines 116–128, trans. Hugh G. Evelyn-White, 1914, *The Internet Sacred Text Archive*, 2008, <http://www.sacred-texts.com/cla/hesiod/theogony.htm> (November 13, 2007).

Chapter Notes

2. Aristotle *Metaphysics* I.3, trans. W. D. Ross, *eBooks@Adelaide,* 2007, <http://ebooks.adelaide.edu.au/a/aristotle/metaphysics/> (November 13, 2007).

3. Simplicius *Physics* 24.13, quoted in G. S. Kirk and J. E. Raven, *The Presocratic Philosophers: A Critical History With a Selection of Texts* (Cambridge: Cambridge University Press, 1957), pp. 105–107.

4. Aristotle *On Generation and Corruption* II.5, trans. H. H. Joachim, *University of Virginia Library,* 2001, <http://etext.virginia.edu/toc/modeng/public/AriGeco.html> (December 5, 2007).

5. Aristotle *Physics* I.4, III.4–5, trans. R. P. Hardie and R. K. Gaye, 1994, <http://classics.mit.edu/Aristotle/physics.html> (December 5, 2007).

6. Simplicius *Physics* 24.26, quoted in Kirk and Raven, p. 145.

7. Plutarch, "On the Principle of Cold," *Moralia* XII.947, trans. Harold Cherniss and William Helmbold, Loeb Classical Library (Cambridge, Mass.: Harvard University Press, 1957), Vol. XII.

8. Plato *Cratylus,* trans. Benjamin Jowett, *The Internet Classics Archive,* n.d., <http://classics.mit.edu/Plato/cratylus.html> (December 14, 2007).

9. Clement (Titus Flavius Clemens) of Alexandria *Stromata* V.104, trans. Peter Kirby, *Early Christian Writings,* 2001, <http://www.earlychristianwritings.com/clement.html> (December 14, 2007).

10. Sextus Empiricus *Against the Professors* VII.132, trans. R. G. Bury, Loeb Classical Library (Cambridge, Mass.: Harvard University Press, 1949), Vol. IV.

11. Parmenides *Fragments and Commentary*, ed. and trans. Arthur Fairbanks, 1898, *Hanover Historical Texts Project,* 2007, <http://history.hanover.edu/texts/presoc/parmends.html> (October 2, 2008);

*Stanford Encyclopedia of Philosophy,* s.v. "Parmenides" (by John Palmer), <http://plato.stanford.edu/entries/parmenides/> (October 2, 2008); Kirk and Raven, pp. 263–285.

12. Parmenides fragment 8, quoted in Kirk and Raven, p. 278.

13. Theophrastus *Metaphysics* fragment 6, quoted in Kirk and Raven, p. 280.

14. Kirk and Raven, pp. 280–282.

15. Simplicius *Physics* 180.9, quoted in Kirk and Raven, p. 282.

16. Simplicius *Physics* 25.21, quoted in Kirk and Raven, pp. 329–330.

17. Aristotle *Physics* I.4.

18. Simplicius *Physics* 34.29, quoted in Kirk and Raven, p. 378.

19. Ibid., 164.24, quoted in Kirk and Raven, pp. 372–373.

20. Ibid., 35.14, quoted in Kirk and Raven, pp. 373–374.

## Chapter 3. The First Atomic Theory

1. Aristotle *On Generation and Corruption* I.8.

2. Simplicius *Physics* 28.4, quoted in G. S. Kirk and J. E. Raven, *The Presocratic Philosophers: A Critical History With a Selection of Texts* (Cambridge: Cambridge University Press, 1957), p. 400.

3. Diogenes Laertius, "The Life of Leucippus (section III)," *The Lives and Opinions of Eminent Philosophers,* Book IX, trans. C. D. Yonge, n.d., <http://www.classicpersuasion.org/pw/diogenes/index.htm> (November 13, 2007).

4. Hippolytus of Rome *Refutation of All Heresies* I.13, quoted in Kirk and Raven, p. 411.

5. Simplicius *On the Heavens* 295.11, quoted in Kirk and Raven, pp. 418–419.

6. Aristotle *Metaphysics* I.4.

7. Simplicius *On the Heavens* 242.21, quoted in Kirk and Raven, p. 419.

8. Aristotle *On Generation and Corruption* I.8.

9. Aetius I.3.18, quoted in Kirk and Raven, p. 414.

10. Ibid., I.12.6, quoted in Kirk and Raven, p. 414.

11. Theophrastus *On the Senses* 61, quoted in Kirk and Raven, p. 414.

12. Aetius I.26.2, quoted in Kirk and Raven, p. 413.

## Chapter 4. How Humans Perceive the World

1. Alexander of Aphrodisias *On the Senses* 56.12, quoted in G. S. Kirk and J. E. Raven, *The Presocratic Philosophers: A Critical History With a Selection of Texts* (Cambridge: Cambridge University Press, 1957), p. 422.

2. Theophrastus *On the Senses* 78, quoted in C. C. W. Taylor, *The Atomists: Leucippus and Democritus. Fragments: A Text and Translation With Commentary* (Toronto: University of Toronto Press, 1999), pp. 115–117.

3. Aetius IV.19, quoted in Kirk and Raven, p. 423.

4. Theophrastus *On the Senses* 55, quoted in Taylor, p. 110.

5. Ibid., *On the Senses* 65, p. 113.

6. Sextus Empiricus *Against the Professors* VII.135.

7. Ibid., VII.139.

8. Aristotle *On the Soul* I.2, trans. J. A. Smith, *The Internet Classics Archive*, n.d., <http://classics.mit .edu/Aristotle/soul.html> (January 11, 2008).

## Chapter 5. The Nature of Living Things

1. Andre Laks, "Soul, Sensation, and Thought," in *The Cambridge Companion to Early Greek Philosophy,* ed. A. A. Long (Cambridge: Cambridge University Press, 1999), p. 251.

2. G. S. Kirk and J. E. Raven, *The Presocratic Philosophers: A Critical History With a Selection of Texts* (Cambridge: Cambridge University Press, 1957), p. 159.

3. Aetius I.3.4, quoted in Kirk and Raven, p. 158.

4. Clement (Titus Flavius Clemens) of Alexandria *Stromata* VI.17, trans. Peter Kirby, *Early Christian Writings,* 2001, <http://www.earlychristianwritings.com/clement.html> (December 14, 2007).

5. Stobaeus *Anthology* III.5, quoted in Kirk and Raven, p. 205.

6. Aristotle *On the Soul* I.2, trans. J. A. Smith, *The Internet Classics Archive,* n.d., <http://classics.mit.edu/Aristotle/soul.html> (January 11, 2008).

7. Ibid.

8. Ibid.

9. Kirk and Raven, pp. 420–421.

10. Pseudo-Galen *On Medical Definitions* XIX.449, quoted in C. C. W. Taylor, *The Atomists: Leucippus and Democritus. Fragments: A Text and Translation With Commentary* (Toronto: University of Toronto Press, 1999), p. 7.

11. Aristotle *On the Generation of Animals* IV.1, trans. Arthur Platt, *eBooks@Adelaide,* 2007, <http://text.library.adelaide.edu.au/a/aristotle/generation/> (January 14, 2008).

## Chapter 6. The Evolution of Human Society

1. Hesiod *Works and Days* lines 109–201, trans. Hugh G. Evelyn-White, *The Internet Sacred Text*

*Archive,* 2008, <http://www.sacred-texts.com/cla/hesiod/works.htm> (January 15, 2008).

    2. Lucretius (Titus Lucretius Carus), *On the Nature of the Universe,* trans. R. E. Latham (Baltimore: Penguin Books, 1951), V.

    3. Thomas Cole, *Democritus and the Sources of Greek Anthropology* (Cleveland, Ohio: American Philological Association, 1967), pp. 10–13.

    4. Herodotus, *The History,* trans. David Greene (Chicago: University of Chicago Press, 1987), VII.69.

    5. Nicholas Wade, *Before the Dawn: Recovering the Lost History of Our Ancestors* (New York: The Penguin Press, 2006), pp. 12–13, 72.

    6. Lucretius *De Rerum Natura* V, lines 925–930.

    7. Ibid., lines 935–944.

    8. Ibid., lines 955, 966–968.

    9. John J. Putnam, "The Search for Modern Humans," *National Geographic,* Vol. 174, October 1988, pp. 449, 470–471.

    10. Lucretius *De Rerum Natura* V, lines 1011–1014.

    11. Ibid., lines 1019–1020.

    12. Ibid., lines 1028–1029, 1056–1058.

    13. Michael Pollan, *The Omnivore's Dilemma* (New York: The Penguin Press, 2006), p. 293.

    14. Lucretius *De Rerum Natura* V, lines 1102–1104.

## Chapter 7. Democritus's Impact on the Ancient World

    1. Stobaeus *Anthology* II.9, quoted in G. S. Kirk and J. E. Raven, *The Presocratic Philosophers: A Critical History With a Selection of Texts* (Cambridge: Cambridge University Press, 1957), p. 424.

    2. Ibid., III.40, p. 425.

    3. Kirk and Raven, p. 425.

4. Stobaeus *Anthology* II.31, quoted in C. C. W. Taylor, *The Atomists: Leucippus and Democritus. Fragments: A Text and Translation With Commentary* (Toronto: University of Toronto Press, 1999), p. 21.

5. Ibid., IV.52, quoted in Taylor, p. 51.

6. Leo Rosten, *The Joys of Yiddish* (New York: Pocket Books, 1968), p. 17.

**Abdera**—A city in northeastern Greece (Thrace), birthplace and home of Democritus.

**Abderite**—A person from Abdera. The Athenians considered Abderites to be "hicks from the sticks."

**alpha particle**—The positively charged nucleus of a helium atom, stripped of its electrons.

**Anaxagoras**—Pre-socratic philosopher who taught that matter was made up of "seeds." He was a strong influence on the atomist school of philosophy.

**Anaximander**—A Milesian philosopher, a student of Thales, who taught that the archê of matter is a primal soup he called The Indefinite.

**Anaximenes**—A Milesian philosopher, a student of Anaximander, who taught that the archê of matter is air.

**archê**—A primal substance out of which everything else is formed.

**Aristotle**—Founder of the Peripatetic school of philosophy. He was an avid student of natural science, and also an author of encyclopedic works that recorded the teachings of earlier philosophers, making him a valuable source of information about the Pre-socratic philosophers. His works were commented upon by a number of later philosophers, who also incorporated the teachings of the Pre-socratics.

**ataraxia**—The sort of calm detachment advocated by the Epicurean school of philosophy.

**atomist**—A philosopher who believes that the universe is made up of atoms and void.

**atomos**—The smallest unit of matter, an atom; literally, "incapable of being cut, indivisible."

**compound**—A substance composed of more than one kind of atom, bonded into a molecule.

**Democritus**—Best known and most influential of the atomist philosophers.

**eidola**—Images, the films of atoms that peel off from physical objects and move through the air until they come in contact with the human eye. Singular *eidolon*.

**electron**—A negatively charged particle that orbits the nucleus of an atom.

**element**—A substance composed of only one type of atom. Gold and oxygen are elements.

**Empedocles**—Pluralist Pre-socratic philosopher who taught that the basic four elements were fire, air, water, and earth. He had a tremendous impact on the scientific theories of the Middle Ages.

**Epicureanism**—The philosophy taught by the Hellenistic philosopher Epicurus. It advocated reason, self-control, the pursuit of simple pleasure, and the practice of a calm detachment from the aggravations of life.

**Hegesistratus**—The father of Democritus; a citizen of Abdera.

**Heraclitus**—A Pre-socratic philosopher who believed that the universe is in a state of continual flux. He may have taught that the archê of matter is fire and that the universe is governed by a system of natural laws that he called the logos.

**Hesiod**—Greek poet who preserved Greek myths about the origin of the universe in his poems *Theogony* (*Origin of the Gods*) and *Works and Days*.

**lepton**—One of the basic building blocks of matter. An electron is a type of lepton.

**Leucippus**—Founder of the atomist school of philosophy and the teacher of Democritus.

**logos**—Literally, "word," but can also mean "natural law," or even "divine intelligence."

**magi**—Persian philosophers or wise men, probably students of Zoroastrianism.

**Milesian**—Member of a school of philosophy that began in the city of Miletos in Asia Minor. The Milesian philosophers included Thales, Anaximander, and Anaximenes. They originated the theory of an archê or basic substance from which all matter is formed.

**neutron**—A particle with no electrical charge, found in the nucleus of an atom.

*panta chorei*— "All things flow," one of the teachings of Heraclitus of Ephesus.

**Parmenides**—The founder of the Eleatic school of philosophy. He taught that reality is a single substance that cannot be perceived by the senses, but only by reason.

**philosopher**—Literally, "lover of wisdom"—someone who studies the principles underlying conduct, thought, knowledge, and the nature of the universe.

**pluralist**—Philosopher who believes that the universe is made up not of a single primal substance, but of more than one. The pluralists included the atomists Leucippus and Democritus.

**Pre-socratic**—Before the time of Socrates (469–399 B.C.), the most famous and influential of the Greek philosophers. The teachings of the Pre-socratic philosophers were the foundation upon which the teachings of later schools of philosophy were built.

**proton**—A positively charged particle found in the nucleus of an atom.

**psychê**— "Soul," according to Democritus, the infusion of fire atoms that gives living things the ability to move around and perceive and understand the world around them.

**quark**—One of the basic building blocks of atomic particles. A proton or a neutron contains three quarks.

**Simplicius**—A commentator on Aristotle who lived in the A.D. 500s. He was responsible for, among other things, preserving most of Parmenides' "Way of Truth."

**Thales**—First of the Milesian school of philosophy. He believed that the archê of matter was water.

**Theophrastus**—A student of Aristotle and his successor as the head of the Peripatetic school. His commentaries on Aristotle's works preserve valuable information about the Pre-socratics.

**vortex**—A whirling mass of atoms out of which worlds are formed.

**Xerxes**—King of Persia who invaded Greece in 480 B.C.

**Zeno**—An Eleatic philosopher, a student of Parmenides.

# FURTHER READING

## Books

Johnson, Rebecca L. *Atomic Structure*. Minneapolis, Minn.: Twenty-First Century Books, 2007.

Kidd, J. S. and Renee A. *Querks and Sparks: The Story of Nuclear Power*. New York: Facts on file, 1999.

Miller, Ron. *The Elements*. Minneapolis, Minn.: Twenty-First Century Books, 2004.

Morgan, Sally. *From Greek Atoms to Quarks: Discovering Atoms*. Chicago: Heinemann Library, 2007.

Nardo, Don. *Ancient Philosophers*. San Diego: Lucent Books, 2004.

Oxlade, Chris. *Atoms*. Chicago: Heinemann Library, 2008.

Stille, Darlene R. *Atoms and Molecules: Building Blocks of the Universe*. Minneapolis, Minn.: Compass Point Books, 2007.

# INTERNET ADDRESSES

**Atomic Models Webquest**
http://mhsweb.ci.manchester.ct.us/Library/webquests/
atomicmodels.htm

**All About Atoms**
http://education.jlab.org/atomtour/index.html

**"Democritus of Abdera," The MacTutor History of Mathematics**
http://www-history.mcs.st-and.ac.uk/history/
Biographies/Democritus.html

# INDEX